The Trained Memory

by Warren Hilton

Copyright © 8/26/2015
Jefferson Publication

ISBN-13: 978-1517073305

Printed in the United States of America

Contents

Chapter I

THE ELEMENTS OF MEMORY

Four Special Memory Processes You have learned of the sense-perceptive and judicial processes by which your mind acquires its knowledge of the outside world. You come now to a study of the phenomenon of memory, the instrument by which your mind retains and makes use of its knowledge, the agency that has power to resurrect the buried past or power to enfold us in a Paradise of dreams more perfect than reality.

In the broadest sense, memory is the faculty of the mind by which we (1) *retain*, (2) *recall*, (3) *picture to the mind's eye*, and (4) *recognize* past experiences.

Memory involves, therefore, four elements, *Retention, Recall, Imagination* and *Recognition*.

THE MENTAL TREASURE VAULT AND ITS LOST COMBINATION

Chapter II

THE MENTAL TREASURE VAULT AND ITS LOST COMBINATION

What Everyone Thinks Almost everyone seems to think that we retain in the mind *only* those things that we can voluntarily recall; that memory, in other words, is limited to the power of voluntary reproduction.

This is a profound error. It is an inexcusable error. The daily papers are constantly reporting cases of the lapse and restoration of memory that contain all the elements of underlying truth on this subject.

Causes of Forgetfulness It is plain enough that the memory *seems* decidedly limited in its scope. This is because our power of voluntary recall is decidedly limited.

But it does not follow simply because we are without the power to deliberately recall certain experiences that all mental trace of those experiences is lost to us.

Those experiences that we are unable to recall are those that we disregarded when they occurred because they possessed no special interest for us. They are there, but no mental associations or connections with power to awaken them have arisen in consciousness.

Things are continually happening all around us that we see with but "half an eye." They are in the "fringe" of Seeing with "Half an Eye" consciousness, and we deliberately ignore them. Many more things come to us in the form of sense-impressions that clamorously assail our sense-organs, but no effort of the will is needed to ignore them. We are absolutely impervious to them and unconscious of them because by the selection of our life interests we have closed the doors against them.

In either case, whether in the "fringe" of consciousness or entirely outside of consciousness, these unperceived sensations will be found to be sensory images that have no connection with the present subject of thought. They therefore attract, and we spare them, no part of our attention.

Just as each of our individual sense-organs selects from the multitude of ether vibrations constantly beating upon the surface of the body only those waves to the velocity of which it is attuned, so each one of us as an integral personality selects from the stream of sensory experiences only those particular objects of attention that are in some way related to the present or habitual trend of thought.

The Man on Broadway Just consider for a moment the countless number and variety of impressions that assail the eye and ear of the New Yorker who walks down Broadway in a busy hour of the day.

5

Yet to how few of these does he pay the slightest attention. He is in the midst of a cataclysm of sound almost equal to the roar of Niagara and he does not know it.

Waxen Tablets Observe how many objects are right now in the corner of your mind's eye as being within the scope of your vision while your entire attention is apparently absorbed in these lines. You see these other things, and you can look back and realize that you have seen them, but you were not aware of them at the time.

Let two individuals of contrary tastes take a day's outing together. Both may have during the day practically identical sensory images; but each one will come back with an entirely different tale to tell of the day's adventures.

All sensory impressions, somehow or other, leave their faint impress on the waxen tablets of the mind. Few are or can be voluntarily recalled.

Just where and how memories are retained is a mystery. There are theories that represent sensory experiences as actual physiological "impressions" on the cells of the brain. They are, however, nothing but theories, and the manner in which the brain, as the organ of the mind, keeps its record of sensory experiences has never been discovered. Microscopic anatomy has never reached the point where it could identify a particular "idea" with any one "cell" or other part of the brain.

Not How, but How Much For us, the important question is not *how*, but *how much*; *not the manner in which, but the extent to which*, sensory impressions are preserved. Now, all the evidences indicate that *absolutely every impression received upon the sensorium Remembering the Unperceived is indelibly recorded in the mind's substance*. A few instances will serve to illustrate the remarkable power of retention of the human mind.

Sir William Hamilton quotes the following from Coleridge's "Literaria Biographia": "A young woman of four- or five-and-twenty, who could neither read nor write, was seized with a nervous fever, during which, according to the asseverations of all the priests and monks of the neighborhood, she became 'possessed,' and, as it appeared, by a very learned devil. She continued incessantly talking Latin, Greek and Hebrew in very pompous tones, and with most distinct enunciation. Sheets full of her ravings were taken down from her own mouth, and were found to consist of sentences coherent and intelligible each for itself but with little or no connection with each other. Of the Hebrew, a small portion only could be traced to the Bible; the remainder seemed to be in the Rabbinical dialect."

The case was investigated by a physician, who learned that the girl had been a waif and had been taken in charge by a Protestant clergyman when she was nine years old and brought up as his servant. This clergyman had for years been in the habit of walking up and down a passage of his house into which the kitchen door opened and at the same time reading to himself in a loud voice from his favorite book. A considerable number of these books were still in the possession of his niece, who told the physician that her uncle had been a very learned man and an accomplished student of Hebrew. Among the books were found a collection of Rabbinical writings, together with several of the Greek and Latin fathers; and the physician succeeded in identifying so many passages in these books with those taken down at the bed-side of the young woman that there could be no doubt as to the true origin of her learned ravings.

Now, the striking feature of all this, it will be observed, is the fact that the subject was an illiterate servant-girl to whom the Greek, Latin and Hebrew quotations were *utterly unintelligible,* that *normally she had no recollection of them, that she had no idea of their Speaking a Forgotten Tongue meaning*, and finally that they had been impressed upon her mind *without her knowledge* while she was engaged in her duties in her master's kitchen.

Several cases are reported by Dr. Abercrombie, and quoted by Professor Hyslop, in which mental impressions long since forgotten beyond the power of voluntary recall have been revived by the shock of accident or disease. "A man," he says, "mentioned by Mr. Abernethy, had been born in France, but had spent the greater part of his life in England, and, for many years, had entirely lost the habit of speaking French. But when under the care of Mr. Abernethy, on account of the effects of an injury to the head, he always spoke French.

"A similar case occurred in St. Thomas Hospital, of a man who was in a state of stupor in consequence of an injury to the head. On his partial recovery he spoke a language which nobody in the hospital understood but which was soon ascertained to be Welsh. It was then discovered that he had been thirty years absent from Wales, and, before the accident, had entirely forgotten his native language.

"A lady mentioned by Dr. Pritchard, when in a state of delirium, spoke a language which nobody about her understood, but which was afterward discovered to be Welsh. None of her friends could form any conception of the manner in which she had become acquainted with that language; but, Living Past Experiences Over Again after much inquiry, it was discovered that in her childhood she had a nurse, a native of a district on the coast of Brittany, the dialect of which is closely analogous to Welsh. The lady at that time learned a good deal of this dialect but had entirely forgotten it for many years before this attack of fever."

Dr. Carpenter relates the following incident in his "Mental Physiology": "Several years ago, the Rev. S. Mansard, now rector of Bethnal Green, was doing clerical duty for a time at Hurstmonceaux, in Sussex; and while there he one day went over with a party of friends to Pevensey Castle, which he did not remember to have ever previously visited. As he approached the gateway he became conscious of a very vivid impression of having seen it before; and he 'seemed to himself to see' not only the gateway itself, but donkeys beneath the arch and people on top of it. His conviction that he must have visited the castle on some former occasion—although he had neither the slightest remembrance of such a visit nor any knowledge of having ever been in the neighborhood previously to his residence at Hurstmonceaux—made him inquire from his mother if she could throw any light on the matter. She at once informed him that being in that part of the country, when he was but *eighteen months old*, she had gone over with a large party and had taken him in the pannier of a donkey; that the elders of the party, having brought lunch with them, had eaten it on the roof of the gateway, where they would have been seen from below, whilst he had been left on the ground with the attendants and donkeys."

"An Italian gentleman," says Dr. Rush, of Philadelphia, "who died of yellow fever in New York, in the beginning of his illness spoke English, in the middle of it French, but on the day of his death only Italian."

Striking as these instances are, they are not unusual. Everyone on reflection can supply similar instances. Who among us has not at one time or another been impressed with a mysterious feeling of having at some time in the past gone through the identical experience which he is living now?

The "Flash of Inspiration" On such occasions the sense of familiarity is sometimes so persistent as to fill one with a strange feeling of the supernatural and to incline our minds to the belief in a reincarnation.

The "flash of inspiration" which, for the lawyer, solves a novel legal issue arising in the trial of a case, or, for the surgeon, sees him successfully through the emergencies of a delicate operation, has its origin in the forgotten learning of past experience and study.

Succeeding books in this *Course* will bring to light numerous other facts less commonly observed, drawn indeed from the study of abnormal mental states, indicating that we retain a great volume of sense-impressions of whose very recording we are at the time unaware. The Totality of Retention In other words, all the evidences point to the absolute totality of our retention of all sensory experiences. They indicate that every sense-impression you ever received, whether you actually perceived and were conscious of it or not, has been retained and preserved in your memory, and can be "brought to mind" when you understand the proper method of calling it into service.

A vast wealth of facts is stored in the treasure vaults of your mind, but there are certain inner compartments to which you have lost the combination.

The author of "Thoughts on Business" says: "It is a great day in a man's life when he truly begins to discover himself. The latent capacities of every Possibilities of Self-Discovery man are greater than he realizes, and he may find them if he diligently seeks for them. A man may own a tract of land for many years without knowing its value. He may think of it as merely a pasture. But one day he discovers evidences of coal and finds a rich vein beneath his land. While mining and prospecting for coal he discovers deposits of granite. In boring for water he strikes oil. Later he discovers a vein of copper ore, and after that silver and gold. These things were there all the time—even when he thought of his land merely as a pasture. But they have a value only when they are discovered and utilized."

"Not every pasture contains deposits of silver and gold, neither oil nor "Acres of Diamonds" granite, nor even coal. But beneath the surface of every man there must be, in the nature of things, a latent capacity greater than has yet been discovered. And one discovery must lead to another until the man finds the deep wealth of his own possibilities. History is full of the acts of men who discovered somewhat of their own capacity; but history has yet to record the man who fully discovered all that he might have been."

You who are a bit vain of your visits to other lands, your wide reading, your experience of men and things; you who secretly lament that so little of what you have seen and read remains with you, behold, your "acres of diamonds" are within you, needing but the mystic formula that shall reveal the treasure!

THE MECHANISM OF RECALL

Chapter III

THE MECHANISM OF RECALL

The Right Stimulus Somehow, somewhere, all experiences, whether subject to voluntary recall or not, are preserved, and are capable of reproduction when the right stimulus comes along.

And it is a law that *those experiences which are associated with each other, whether ideas, emotions or voluntary or involuntary muscular movements, tend to become bound together into groups, and these groups tend to become bound together into systems.*

"Complexes" of Experience Such a system of associated groups of experiences is technically known as a "complex."

Pay particular attention to these definitions, as "groups" of ideas and "complexes" of ideas, emotions and muscular movements are terms that we shall constantly employ.

You learned in a former lesson that mental experiences may consist not only of sense-perceptions based on excitements arising in the memory nerves, but also of bodily emotions, the "feeling tones" of ideas, and of muscular movements based on stimuli arising in the motor nerves.

11

Groups consist, therefore, not only of associated ideas, but of associated ideas coupled with their emotional The Thrill of Recollection qualities and impulses to muscular movements.

All groups bound together by a mutually related idea constitute a single "complex." Every memory you have is an illustration of such "complexes."

Suppose, for example, you once gained success in a business deal. Your recollection of the other persons concerned in that transaction, of any one detail in the transaction itself, will be accompanied by the faster heartbeat, the quickened circulation of the blood, the feeling of triumph and elation that attended the original experience.

Complexes formed out of harrowing earthquakes, robberies, murders or other dreadful spectacles, which were originally accompanied on the part of "Complexes" and Functional Derangements the onlooker by trembling, perspiration and palpitation of the heart, when lived over again in memory, are again accompanied by all these bodily activities. Your memory of a hairbreadth escape will bring to your cheek the pallor that marked it when the incident occurred.

The formation and existence of "complexes" explains the origin of many functional diseases of the body—that is to say, diseases involving no loss or destruction of tissue, but consisting simply in a failure on the part of some bodily organ to perform its allotted function naturally and effectively.

Thus, in hay fever or "rose cold" the tears, the inflammation of the membranes of the nose, the cough, the other trying symptoms, all are linked with Automatically Working Mental Mechanisms the sight of a rose, or dust, or sunlight, or some other outside fact to which attention has been called as the cause of hay fever, into a complex, "an automatically working mechanism." And the validity of this explanation of the regular recurrence of attacks of this disease is sufficiently demonstrated by the fact that a paper rose is likely to prove just as effective in producing all the symptoms of the disease as a rose out of Nature's garden.

Another striking illustration of the working of this principle is afforded by two gentlemen of my acquaintance, brothers, each of whom since boyhood has had unfailing attacks of sneezing upon first arising in the morning. No sooner is one of these men awake and Two Classes of "Complexes" seated upon the edge of his bed for dressing than he begins to sneeze, and he continues to sneeze for fifteen or twenty minutes thereafter, although he has no "cold" and never sneezes at any other time.

Obviously, if absolutely all mental experiences are preserved, they consist altogether of two broad classes of complexes: first, those that are momentarily *active in consciousness*, forming part of the present mental picture, and, second, all the others—that is to say, all past experiences that are *not at the present moment before the mind's eye*.

There are, then, *conscious* complexes and *subconscious* complexes, complexes of *consciousness* and complexes of *subconsciousness*.

 The Subconscious Storehouse And of the complexes of subconsciousness, some are far more readily recalled than others. Some are forever popping into one's thoughts, while others can be brought to the light of consciousness only by some unusual and deep-probing stimulus. And *the human mind is a vast storehouse of complexes, far the greater part buried in subconsciousness*, yet somehow, like impressions on the wax cylinder of a phonograph, preserved with life-like truth and clearness.

Turn back for a moment to our definition of memory. You will observe that its second essential element is Recall.

Recall is the process by which the experiences of the past are summoned from the reservoir of the subconscious into the light of present consciousness. We necessarily touched upon this process in a previous book, in considering the Laws of Association, but here, in relation to memory, we shall go into the matter somewhat more analytically.

THE LAWS OF RECALL

Chapter IV

THE LAWS OF RECALL

The Law of Integral Recall Law I. The primary law of recall is this: *The recurrence or stimulation of one element in a complex tends to recall all the others.*

In our explanation of "complex" formation we necessarily cited instances that illustrate this principle as well, since *recall is merely a reverse operation from that involved in "complex" formation.*

For example, in running through a book I come upon a flower pressed between its pages. At once the memory What Ordinary "Thinking" Amounts to of the friend who gave it to me springs into consciousness and becomes the subject of reminiscence. This recalls the mountain village where we last met. This recalls the fact that a railroad was at the time under process of construction, which should transform the village into a popular resort. This in turn suggests my coming trip to the seashore, and I am reminded of a business appointment on which my ability to leave town on the appointed day depends. And so on indefinitely.

Far the greater part of your successive states of consciousness, or even of your ordinary "thinking," commonly so-called, consists of trains of mental pictures "suggested" one by another. If the associated pictures are of the everyday The Reverse of Complex Formation type, common to everyone, you have a prosaic mind; if, on the other hand, the associations are unusual or unique, you are happily possessed of wit and fancy.

These instances of the action of the Law of Recall illustrate but one phase of its activity. They show simply that groups of ideas are so strung together on the string of some common element that *the activity of one "group" in consciousness is apt to be automatically followed by the others. But the law of association goes deeper than this. It enters into the activity of every individual group, and causes all the elements of every group, ideas, emotions and impulses to muscular movements, to be simultaneously manifested.*

Prolixity and Terseness There is no principle to which we shall more continually refer than this one. Our explanation of hay fever a moment ago illustrates our meaning. Get the principle clearly in your mind, and see how many instances of its operation you can yourself supply from your own daily experience.

So far as the mere linking together of groups of ideas is concerned, this classifying quality is developed in some persons to a greater degree than in others. It finds its extreme exemplar in the type of man who can never relate an incident without reciting all the prolix and minute details and at the same time wandering far from the original subject in pursuit of every suggested idea.

The Law of Contiguity Law II. *Similarity and nearness in time or space between two experiential facts causes the thought of one to tend to recall the thought of the other.*

This is the Associative Law of Contiguity considered from the standpoint of recall. The points of contiguity are different for different individuals. Similarities and nearnesses will awaken all sorts of associated groups of ideas in one person that are not at all excitable in the same way in another whose experiences have been different.

Law III. *The greater the frequency and intensity of any given experience, the greater the ease and likelihood of its reproduction and recall.*

This explains why certain groups in Laws of Habit and Intensity any complex are more readily recalled than others—why some leap forth unbidden, why some come next and before others, why some arrive but tardily or not at all.

This is how the associative Laws of Habit and Intensity affect the power of recall.

There is no department of business to which the application of these Laws of Recall is so apparent as the department of advertising. The most carefully worded and best-illustrated advertisement may fail to pay its cost unless the underlying principles of choice of position, selection of medium and size of space are understood. The advertisers in metropolitan newspapers Applications to Advertising and magazines of large circulation are the ones who have most at stake. But whatever the field to be reached, it is well to bear in mind certain facts based on the Laws of Recall that have been established by psychological experiment.

Most advertisers have a general idea that certain relative positions on the newspaper or magazine page are to be preferred over others, but they have no conception of the real differences in relative recall value. When the great cost of space in large publications is considered the financial value of such knowledge is evident.

By a great number of tests the relative recall value of every part of the newspaper page has been approximately Effect of Repetitions determined. It has been found, for example, that a given space at the upper right-hand corner of the page has more than twice the value of the same amount of space in the lower left-hand corner.

Many advertisers adopt the policy of repeating full-page advertisements at long intervals instead of advertising in a small way continually. Laboratory tests have shown, on the contrary, that a quarter-page advertisement appearing in four successive issues of a newspaper is fifty per cent more effective than a full-page advertisement appearing only once. It does not follow, however, that an eighth-page advertisement repeated eight times is correspondingly more effective; for below a certain relative size the value of an advertisement Ratio of Size to Value decreases much more rapidly than the cost. There are, of course, modifying conditions, such as special sales of department stores, where occasional displays and announcements make it desirable to use either full pages, or even double pages, but the great bulk of advertising is not of this character.

Every year in the United States alone six hundred millions of dollars are expended in advertising the sale of commodities, and for the most part expended in a haphazard, experimental and unscientific way. The investment of this vast sum with risk of perhaps total loss, or even possible injury, through the faulty construction or improper placing of advertisements should stimulate the interest of every Risks in Advertising advertiser in the work that psychologists have done and are doing toward the accumulation of a body of exact knowledge on this subject.

THE SCIENCE OF FORGETTING

TESTING THE MEMORY

Chapter V

THE SCIENCE OF FORGETTING

The Skilled Artisan Attention is the instrumentality through which the Laws of Recall operate. Wittingly or unwittingly, consciously or unconsciously, every man's attention swings in automatic obedience to the Laws of Recall.

Attention is the artisan that, bit by bit, and with lightning quickness, constructs the mosaic of consciousness.

Having the whole vast store of all present and past experiences to draw upon, he selects only those groups and How the Attention Works those isolated instances that are related to our general interests and aims. He disregards others.

The attention operates in a manner complementary to the general Laws of Recall. It is an active principle not of association, but of *dissociation.*

You choose, for example, a certain aim in life. You decide to become the inventor of an aeroplane of automatic stability. This choice henceforth determines two things. First, it determines just which of the sensory experiences of any given moment are most likely to be selected for your conscious perception. Secondly, it determines just which of your past experiences will be most likely to be recalled.

Such a choice, in other words, determines Iron Filings and Mental Magnets to some extent the sort of elements that will most probably be selected to make up at any moment the contents of your consciousness.

From the instant that you make such a choice you are on the alert for facts relevant to the subject of your ambition. Upon them you concentrate your attention. They are presented to your consciousness with greater precision and clearness than other facts. All facts that pertain to the art of flying henceforth cluster and cling to your conscious memory like iron filings to a magnet. All that are impertinent to this main pursuit are dissociated from these intensely active complexes, and in time fade into subconscious forgetfulness.

By subconscious forgetfulness we The Compartment of Subconscious Forgetfulness mean a *compartment*, as it were, of that reservoir in which all past experiences are stored.

Consciousness is a momentary thing. It is a passing state. It is ephemeral and flitting. It is made up *in part of present sense-impressions* and in part of past experiences. These past experiences

19

are brought forth from subconsciousness. Some are voluntarily brought forth. Some present themselves without our conscious volition, but by the operation of the laws of association and dissociation. Some we seem unable voluntarily to recall, yet they may appear when least we are expecting them. It is these last to which we have referred as lost in subconscious forgetfulness. As a matter of fact, *none* are ever actually *lost*.

Making Experience Count All the wealth of your past experience is still yours—a concrete part of your personality. All that is required to make it available for your present use is a sufficient concentration of your attention, *a concentration of attention that shall dwell persistently and exclusively upon those associations that bear upon the fact desired.*

The tendency of the mind toward dissociation, a function limiting the indiscriminate recall of associated "groups," is also manifested in all of us in the transfer to unconsciousness of many *muscular activities.*

As infants we learn to walk only by giving to every movement of the limbs the most deliberate conscious attention. Yet, in time, the complicated co-operation How Habits Are Formed of muscular movements involved in walking becomes involuntary and unconscious, so that we are no longer even aware of them.

It is the same with reading, writing, playing upon musical instruments, the manipulation of all sorts of mechanical devices, the thousand and one other muscular activities that become what we call *habitual.*

The moment one tries to make these habitual activities again dependent on the conscious will he encounters difficulties.

"The centipede was happy quite, Until the toad, for fun, Said, 'Pray which leg goes after which?' This stirred his mind to such a pitch, He lay distracted in a ditch, Considering *how* to run."

All these habitual activities are started as acts of painstaking care and conscious attention. All ultimately become unconscious. They may, however, be started or stopped at will. They are, therefore, still related to the conscious mind. They occupy a semi-automatic middle ground between conscious and subconscious activities.

THE FALLACY OF MOST MEMORY SYSTEMS

Chapter VI

THE FALLACY OF MOST MEMORY SYSTEMS

Practice in Memorizing Inadequate It is evident that if what we have been describing as the process of recall is true, then the commonly accepted idea that *practice* in memorizing makes memorizing *easier* is false, and that there is no truth in the popular figure of speech that likens the memory to a muscle that grows stronger with use.

So far as the memory is concerned, however, practice may result in a more or less unconscious improvement in the *methods* of memorizing.

Torture of the Drill *By practice we come to unconsciously discover and employ new associative methods in our recording of facts, making them easier to recall, but we can certainly add nothing to the actual scope and power of retention.*

Yet many books on memory-training have wide circulation whose authors, showing no conception of the processes involved, seek to develop the general ability to remember by incessant practice in memorizing particular facts, just as one would develop a muscle by exercise.

The following is quoted from a well-known work of this character:

"I am now treating a case of loss of memory in a person advanced in years, who did not know that his memory had failed most remarkably until I told him of it. He is making vigorous efforts to bring it back again, and with partial success. The method pursued is to spend two hours daily, one in the morning and one in the evening, in exercising this faculty. The patient is instructed to give the closest attention to all that he learns, so that it shall be impressed on his mind clearly. He is asked to recall every evening all the facts and experiences of the day, and again the next morning. Every name heard is written down and impressed on his mind clearly and an effort made to recall it at intervals. Ten names from among public men are ordered to be committed to memory every week. A verse of poetry is to be learned, also a Real Cause of Failing Memory verse from the Bible, daily. He is asked to remember the number of the page of any book where any interesting fact is recorded. These and *other* methods are slowly resuscitating a failing memory."

As remarked by Professor James, "It is hard to believe that the memory of the poor old gentleman is a bit the better for all this torture except in respect to the particular facts thus wrought into it, the occurrences attended to and repeated on those days, the names of those politicians, those Bible verses, etc., etc."

The error in the book first quoted from lies in the fact that its author looks upon a failing memory as indicating a loss of retentiveness. The *real* cause is the loss of an intensity of interest. *It is the failure to form sufficiently large The Manufactured Interest groups and complexes of related ideas, emotions and muscular movements associated with the particular fact to be remembered. There is no reason to believe that the retention of sensory experiences is not at all times perfectly mechanical and mechanically perfect.*

Interest is a mental yearning. It is the offspring of desire and the mother of memory.

It goes out spontaneously to anything that can add to the sum of one's knowledge about the thing desired.

A manufactured interest is counterfeit. When a thing is done because it has to be done, desire dies and "duty" is born. In proportion as a subject is associated with "duty," it is divorced from interest.

Memory Lure of a Desire If you want to impress anything on another man's mind so that he will remember it, harness it up with the lure of a desire.

Diffused interest is the cause of all unprofitable forgetfulness. Do not allow your attention to grope vaguely among a number of things. Whatever you do, make a business of doing it with your whole soul. Turn the spotlight of your mind upon it, and you will not forget it.

TESTING ABILITY TO OBSERVE, REMEMBER AND REPORT THINGS SEEN

A SCIENTIFIC MEMORY SYSTEM FOR BUSINESS SUCCESS

Chapter VII

A SCIENTIFIC MEMORY SYSTEM FOR BUSINESS SUCCESS

Importance of Associates We recall things by their associates. *When you set your mind to remember any particular fact, your conscious effort should be not vaguely to will that it shall be impressed and retained, but analytically and deliberately to connect it with one or more other facts already in your mind.*

The student who "crams" for an examination makes no permanent addition "Cramming" and "Willing" to his knowledge. There can be no recall without association, and "cramming" allows no time to form associations.

If you find it difficult to remember a fact or a name, do not waste your energies in "willing" it to return. Try to recall some other fact or name associated with the first in time or place or otherwise, and lo! when you least expect it, it will pop into your thoughts.

If your memory is good in most respects, but poor in a particular line, it is because you do not interest yourself in that line, and therefore have no material for association. Blind Tom's memory was a blank on most subjects, but he was a walking encyclopedia on music.

 Basic Principle of Thought-Reproduction *To improve your memory you must increase the number and variety of your mental associations.*

Many ingenious methods, scientifically correct, have been devised to aid in the remembering of particular facts. These methods are based wholly on the principle that *that is most easily recalled which is associated in our minds with the most complex and elaborate groupings of related ideas.*

Thus, Pick, in "Memory and Its Doctors," among other devices, presents a well-known "figure-alphabet" as of aid in remembering numbers. Each figure of the Arabic notation is represented by one or more letters, and the number to be recalled is translated into such letters as can best be arranged Methods of Pick into a catch word or phrase. To quote: "The most common figure-alphabet is this:

25

```
:  :  3  ʌ  !  6  7  ೭  ৎ  (

t  ſ  ᴨ  ſ  l   ˢ     g   f   ⊦  ৎ
            h

(              j   k   \  ⊦  (

            c
                c
         h

            q
         g      ಌ
         u
```

"To briefly show its use, suppose it is desired to fix 1,142 feet in a second as the velocity of sound, t, t, r, n, are the letters and order required. Fill up with vowels forming a phrase like 'tight run' and connect it by some such flight of the imagination as that if a man tried to keep up with the velocity of sound, he would have a 'tight run.'"

The same principle is at the basis of all efficient pedagogy. The competent Scientific Pedagogy teacher endeavors by some association of ideas to link every new fact with those facts which the pupil already has acquired.

In the pursuit of this method the teacher will "compare all that is far off and foreign to something that is near home, making the unknown plain by the example of the known, and connecting all the instruction with the personal experience of the pupil—if the teacher is to explain the distance of the sun from the earth, let him ask, 'If anyone there in the sun fired off a cannon straight at you, what should you do?' 'Get out of the way,' would be the answer. 'No need of that,' the teacher might reply; 'you may quietly go to sleep in your room and get up How to Remember Names again; you may wait till your confirmation day, you may learn a trade, and grow as old as I am—*then only* will the cannon-ball be getting near, *then* you may jump to one side! See, so great as that is the sun's distance!'"

We shall now show you how to apply this principle in improving your memory and in making a more complete use of your really vast store of knowledge.

Rule I. *Make systematic use of your sense-organs.*

Do you find it difficult to remember names? It is because you do not link them in your mind with enough associations. Every time a man is introduced to you, look about you. Who is present? Take note of as many and as great a variety of surrounding facts and circumstances as possible. Think of the man's name, and take another look at his face, his dress, his physique. Think of his name, and at the same time his voice and manner. Think of his name, and mark the place where you are now for the first time meeting him. Think of his name in conjunction with the name and personality of the friend who presented him.

Memory is not a distinct faculty of mind in the sense that one man is generously endowed in that respect while another is deficient. Memory, as meaning the power of voluntary recall, is wholly a question of trained habits of mental operation.

Five Exercises for Developing Observation Your memory is just as good as mine or any other man's. It is your indifference to what you would call "irrelevant facts" that is at fault. Therefore, cultivate habits of observation. Fortify the observed facts you wish to recall with a multitude of outside associations. Never rest with a mere halfway knowledge of things.

To assist you in training yourself in those habits of observation that make a good memory of outside facts, we append the following exercises:

a. Walk slowly through a room with which you are not familiar. Then make a list of all the contents of the room you can recall. Do this every day for a week, using a different room each time. Do it not half-heartedly, but as if your life depended on your ability to remember. At the end of the week you will be surprised at the improvement you have made.

b. As you walk along the street, observe all that occurs in a space of one block, things heard as well as things seen. Two hours later make a list of all you can recall. Do this twice a day for ten days. Then compare results.

c. Make a practice of recounting each night the incidents of the day. The prospect of having this to do will cause you unconsciously to observe more attentively.

This is the method by which Thurlow Weed acquired his phenomenal memory. As a young man with political ambitions he had been much troubled by his inability to recall names and faces. So he began the practice each night of telling his wife the most minute details of incidents that had occurred during the day. He kept this up for fifty years, and it so trained his powers of observation that he became as well known for his unfailing memory as for his political adroitness.

d. Glance once at an outline map of some State. Put it out of sight and draw one as nearly like it as you can. Then compare it with the original. Do this frequently.

e. Have some one read you a sentence out of a book and you then repeat it. Do this daily, gradually increasing the length of the quotation from short sentences to whole paragraphs. Try to Invention and Thought-Memory find out what is the extreme limit of your ability in this respect compared with that of other members of your family.

Rule II. *Fix ideas by their associates.*

There are other things to be remembered besides facts of outside observation. You are not one whose life is passed entirely in a physical world. You live also within. Your mind is unceasingly at work with the materials of the past painting the pictures of the future. You are called upon to scheme, to plan, to devise, to invent, to compose and to foresee.

If all this mental work is not wasted energy, you must be able to recall its Three Exercises for Developing Thought-Memory conclusions when occasion requires. A happy thought comes to you—will you remember it tomorrow when the hour for action arrives? There is but one way to be sure, and that is by making a study of the whole associative mental process.

Review the train of ideas by which you reached your conclusion. Carry the thought on in mind to its legitimate conclusion. See yourself acting upon it. Mark its relations to other persons. Note all the details of the mental picture. In other words, to remember thoughts, cultivate thought-observation just as you cultivate sense-observation to remember outside matters.

To train yourself in thought-memory, use the following exercises:

a. Every morning at eight o'clock, sharp on the minute, fix upon a certain idea and determine to recall it at a certain hour during the day. Put your whole will into this resolution. Try to imagine what activities you will be engaged in at the appointed hour, and think of the chosen idea as identified with those activities. Associate it in your mind with some object that will be at hand when the set time comes. Having thus fixed the idea in your mind, forget it. Do not refer to it in your thoughts. With practice you will find yourself automatically carrying out your own orders. Persist in this exercise for at least three months.

b. Every night when you retire fix upon the hour at which you wish to get up in the morning. In connection with your waking at that hour, think of all the sounds that will be apt to be occurring at that particular time. Bar every other thought from your consciousness and fall asleep with the intense determination to arise at the time set. By all means, get up instantly when you awaken. Keep up this exercise and you will soon be able to awaken at any hour you may wish.

c. Every morning outline the general plan of your activities for the day. Select only the important things. Do not bother with the details. Determine upon the logical order for your day's work. Think not so much of *how* you are to do things as of the *things* you are to do. Keep your mind on results. And How to Compel Recollection having made your plan, stick to it. Be your own boss. Let nothing tempt you from your set purpose. Make this daily planning a habit and hold to it through life. It will give you a great lift toward whatever prize you seek.

Rule III. *Search systematically and persistently.*

When once you have started upon an effort at recollection, persevere. The date or face or event that you wish to recall *is bound up with a multitude of other facts of observation and of your mind life* of the past. Success in recalling it depends simply upon your ability *to hit upon some idea so indissolubly associated with the object of search that the recall of one automatically recalls Formation of Correct Memory Habits the other.* Consequently the thing to do is to hold your attention to one definite line of thought until you have exhausted its possibilities. You must pass in review all the associated matters and suppress or ignore them until the right one comes to mind. This may be a short-cut process or a roundabout process, but it will bring results nine times out of ten, and if habitually persisted in will greatly improve your power of voluntary recall.

Rule IV. *The instant you recollect a thing to be done, do it.*

Every idea that memory thrusts into your consciousness carries with it the impulse to act upon it. If you fail to do so, the matter may not again occur NOW! to you, or when it does it may be too late.

Your mental mechanism will serve you faithfully only as long as you act upon its suggestions.

This is as true of bodily habits as of business affairs. The time to act upon an important matter that just now comes to mind is not "tomorrow" or a "little later," but *NOW*.

What you do from moment to moment tells the story of your career. Ideas that come to you should be compared as to their relative importance. But do this honestly. Do not be swayed by distracting impulses that inadvertently slip in. And having gauged their importance give free rein at once to the impulse to do everything that Persistence, Accuracy, Dispatch should not make way for something more important.

If, for any reason, action must be deferred, fix the matter in your mind to be called up at the proper time. Drive all other thoughts from your consciousness. Give your whole attention to this one matter. Determine the exact moment at which you wish it to be recalled. Then put your whole self into the determination to remember it at precisely the right moment. And finally, and perhaps most important of all,—

Rule V. *Have some sign or token.* This memory signal may be anything you choose, but it must somehow be directly connected with the hour at which the main event is to be recalled.

Make a business of observing the Memory Signs and Tokens memory signs or tokens you have been habitually using. Practice tagging those matters you wish to recall with the labels that form a part of your mental machinery.

Make it a habit to do things when they ought to be done and in the order in which you ought to do them. Habits like this are "paths" along which the mind "moves," paths of least resistance to those qualities of promptness, energy, persistence, accuracy, self-control, and so on, that create success.

Success in business, success in life, can come only through the formation of right habits. A right habit can be deliberately acquired only by *doing a thing consciously until it comes to be done unconsciously and automatically*.

The Mental Combination Revealed Every man, consciously or unconsciously, forms his own memory habits, good or bad. Form your memory habits consciously according to the laws of the mind, and in good time they will act unconsciously and with masterful precision.

"'Amid the shadows of the pyramids,' Bonaparte said to his soldiers, 'twenty centuries look down upon you,' and animated them to action and victory. But all the centuries," says W.H. Grove, "and the eternities, and God, and the universe, look down upon us—and demand the highest culture of body, mind and spirit."

A good memory is yours for the making. But *you* must make it. We can point the way. *You* must act.

The laws of Association and Recall are the combination that will unlock the treasure-vaults of memory. Apply these laws, and the riches of experience will be available to you in every need.

The purpose of this book has been to make clear certain mental principles and processes, namely, those of Retention, Association and Recall. Incidentally, as with every book in this *Course*, it contains some facts and instructions of immediate practical utility. But primarily it is intended only to help prepare your mind to understand a scientific system for success-achievement that will be unfolded in subsequent volumes.